INCREDIBLE
SPORTS
RECORDS

SOCCER

RECORDS

BY THOMAS K. ADAMSON

BLASTOFF!
DISCOVERY

Bellwether Media • Minneapolis, MN

Blastoff! Discovery launches
a new mission: reading to learn.
Filled with facts and features,
each book offers you an exciting
new world to explore!

This edition first published in 2018 by Bellwether Media, Inc.

No part of this publication may be reproduced in whole or in
part without written permission of the publisher. For information
regarding permission, write to Bellwether Media, Inc., Attention:
Permissions Department, 5357 Penn Avenue South, Minneapolis,
MN, 55419.

Library of Congress Cataloging-in-Publication Data

Names: Adamson, Thomas K., 1970- author.
Title: Soccer Records / by Thomas K. Adamson.
Description: Minneapolis, MN : Bellwether Media, Inc., 2018.
   | Series: Blastoff! Discovery: Incredible Sports Records |
   Includes bibliographical references and index. |
   Audience: Age 7-13. | Audience: 3-8.
Identifiers: LCCN 2017033110 (print) |
   LCCN 2017046862 (ebook) | ISBN
   9781626177864 (hardcover : alk. paper |
   ISBN 9781681034973 (ebook)) |
   ISBN 9781618913166 (pbk. : alk. paper)
Subjects: LCSH: Soccer–Records–Juvenile literature. |
   Soccer–History–Juvenile literature.
Classification: LCC GV943.25 (ebook) | LCC GV943.25 .A38
   2018 (print) | DDC 796.334–dc23
LC record available at https://lccn.loc.gov/2017033110

Editor: Nathan Sommer   Designer: Steve Porter

Printed in the United States of America, North Mankato, MN.

TABLE OF CONTENTS

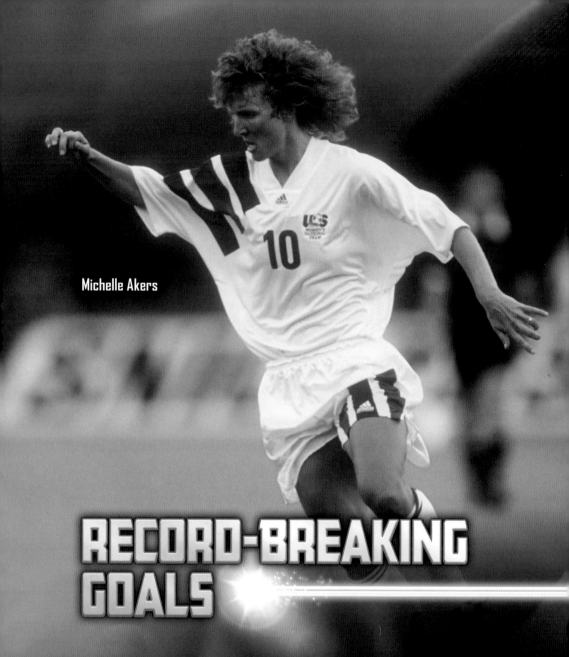

Michelle Akers

RECORD-BREAKING GOALS

The United States team made its dominance in soccer clear at the first Women's World Cup. Led by Carin Jennings and Michelle Akers, the team went undefeated to become champions. On November 24, 1991, Akers made history. She scored an unbelievable five **goals** against Taiwan.

No other player has scored as many goals in a Women's Cup match. Accomplishments like this are what make the competition so popular worldwide. Read on to learn about other incredible World Cup records!

RECORD-BREAKING PLAYERS

The World Cup has turned many great players into icons. Its competitors have set some amazing records over the years.

Miroslav Klose was a scoring weapon for Germany in four World Cups. In 2014, he scored his 16th career goal at the event. This helped Germany win the Cup and broke the record for most career goals scored!

LUCKY CHARM

Germany's World Cup team never lost a game in which Miroslav Klose scored.

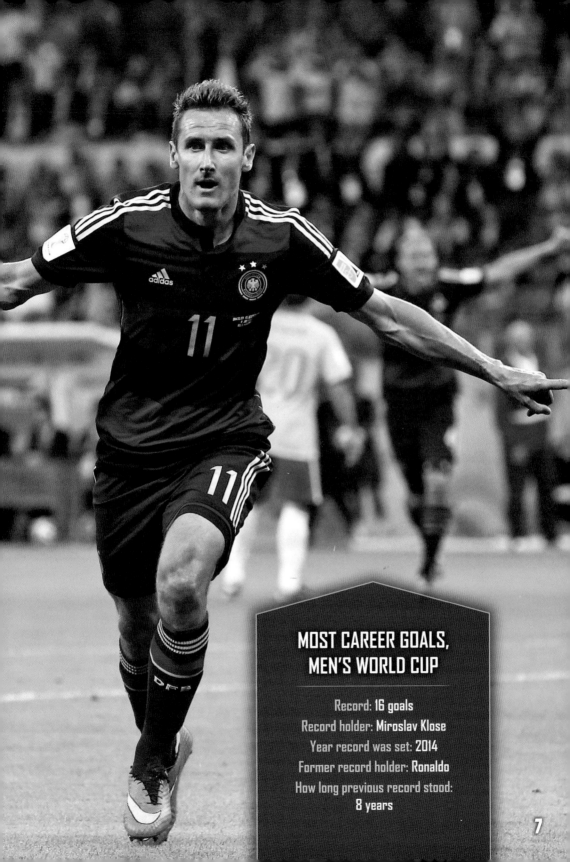

MOST CAREER GOALS, MEN'S WORLD CUP

Record: 16 goals
Record holder: Miroslav Klose
Year record was set: 2014
Former record holder: Ronaldo
How long previous record stood:
8 years

France's Just Fontaine holds a World Cup record that might remain unbroken forever. He scored a record 13 goals at the 1958 **tournament**. It was the only Cup Fontaine played in, but his 13 career goals are enough to be fourth-highest in the event's history!

LATE ENTRY

Fontaine was not even an original member of France's team in 1958! He was added to it last minute to replace an injured player.

MOST GOALS AT ONE MEN'S WORLD CUP

Record: 13 goals
Record holder: Just Fontaine
Year record was set: 1958
Former record holder:
Sándor Kocsis
How long previous record stood:
4 years

MOST CAREER GOALS, WOMEN'S WORLD CUP

Record: 15 goals
Record holder: **Marta**
Year record was set: 2015
Former record holder:
Birgit Prinz
How long previous record stood:
8 years

Many consider Marta to be the best player in Women's World Cup history. She scored a record 15 goals over four tournaments, more than any other female player. Her leadership makes Brazil a threat every time she is on the field.

Pelé is also the youngest player ever to score a goal in a final. At age 17, he scored two goals to help Brazil defeat Sweden in its 1958 World Cup victory.

MOST MEN'S WORLD CUP CHAMPIONSHIP WINS

Record: **3 wins**

Record holder: **Pelé**

Year record was set: **1970**

Former record holder:
4 players tied before Pelé

How long previous record stood:
32 years

Pelé is often called the greatest soccer player ever. His name is recognized by fans everywhere. No other player has won as many World Cups as Pelé. His unmatched skills helped Brazil win the championship in 1958, 1962, and 1970!

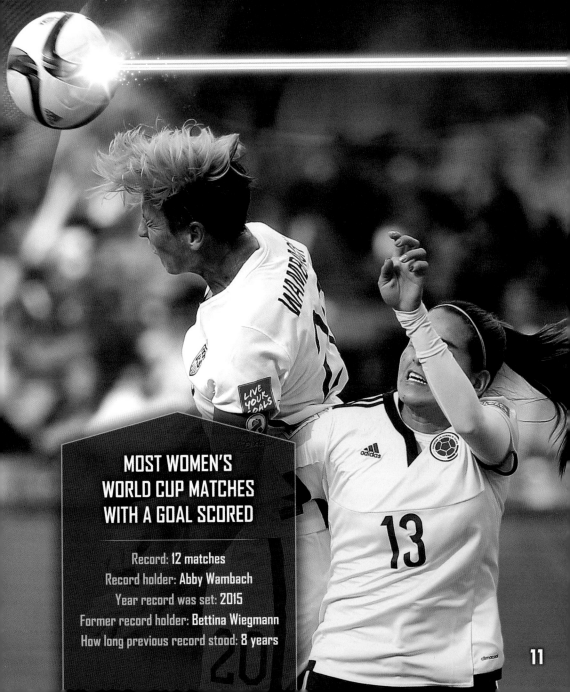

Abby Wambach was a leader on the U.S. women's team for years. She specialized in scoring by **header**. Wambach scored in a record 12 matches over four tournaments. Her fierce playing helped the team win the title in 2015.

MOST WOMEN'S WORLD CUP MATCHES WITH A GOAL SCORED

Record: 12 matches
Record holder: Abby Wambach
Year record was set: 2015
Former record holder: Bettina Wiegmann
How long previous record stood: 8 years

Goalkeepers have had some incredible moments at the World Cup, too. Italy's Walter Zenga proved this in 1990. That year, he played a record 518 **consecutive** minutes without allowing a goal. His opponents went scoreless in five straight matches!

MOST CONSECUTIVE MINUTES WITHOUT ALLOWING A GOAL, MEN'S WORLD CUP

Record: 518 minutes
Record holder: Walter Zenga
Year record was set: 1990
Former record holder: Peter Shilton
How long previous record stood: 4 years

Germany's Nadine Angerer did not allow a single goal at the 2007 Women's Cup. That year, Angerer recorded six **shutouts** before her team won the tournament. This included stopping a **penalty kick** from Brazil's Marta in the final match.

FEWEST GOALS ALLOWED BY A CHAMPION GOALKEEPER, WOMEN'S WORLD CUP

Record: 0 goals
Record holder: Nadine Angerer
Year record was set: 2007
Former record holder: Bente Nordby
How long previous record stood:
12 years

RECORD-BREAKING TEAMS

Exciting teamwork helps make the World Cup the world's most popular sporting event. Winning **streaks** and titles come to the teams who are great at working together. The best break records!

Brazil has made its mark on the Men's World Cup. Superstars like Pelé and Ronaldo have made Brazil's team a force in every tournament. The team has won the Cup a record five times! It is the only team that has played in every Men's Cup.

WIN STREAK

The Brazil men's team strung together 11 straight wins from 2002 to 2006. This broke the record for most consecutive wins in World Cup history!

MOST MEN'S WORLD CUP TITLES

Record: 5 titles

Record holder: Brazil

Year record was set: 2002

Former record holder:
broke their own record

How long previous record stood:
8 years

BIGGEST WORLD CUP WINNERS

The United States women's team also holds the record for most matches won. They have won 43 matches over seven tournaments!

The United States team claims the title of best in Women's World Cup history. The team has won three of the seven tournaments held so far! They are a favorite at every competition.

MOST WOMEN'S WORLD CUP TITLES

Record: 3 titles
Record holder: United States
Year record was set: 2015
Former record holder:
broke their own record
How long previous record stood:
16 years

Germany has been a top scorer at the Men's Cup. Its team holds the record for most total goals scored during the competition. So far, this high-scoring team has scored 224 goals over 18 World Cups!

MOST MEN'S WORLD CUP GOALS SCORED

Record: 224 goals
Record holder: Germany
Year record was set: 2014
Former record holder: Brazil
How long previous record stood:
64 years

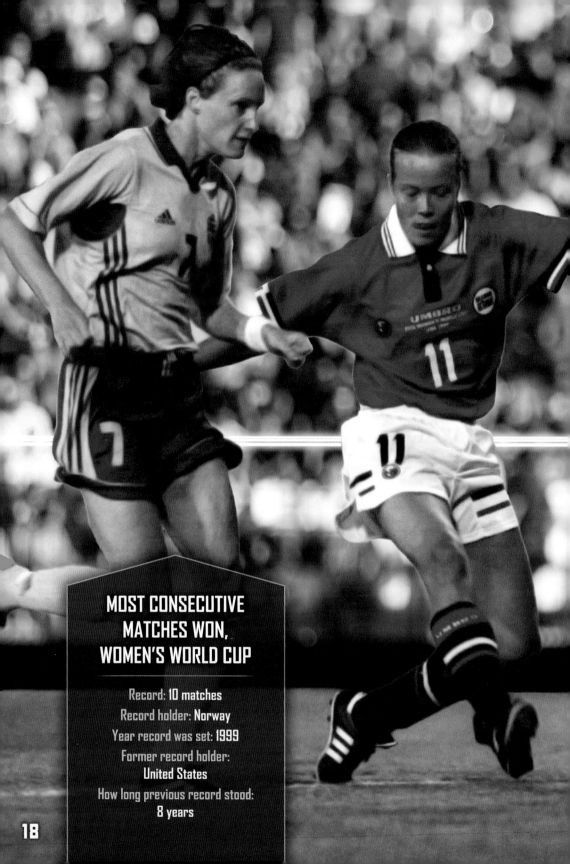

MOST CONSECUTIVE MATCHES WON, WOMEN'S WORLD CUP

Record: 10 matches
Record holder: Norway
Year record was set: 1999
Former record holder:
United States
How long previous record stood:
8 years

The Norway women's team was unstoppable in the 1990s. The team won all six matches to take home the title in 1995. Then, they cruised to victory in their first four matches in 1999. It was the most consecutive wins in Women's Cup history!

The 1954 Hungary men's team is one of the best to never win it all. Masters of scoring, the team averaged a record 5.4 goals per match. Hungary lost that year's final 3–2. But the team's scoring record still remains today!

HIGHEST AVERAGE GOALS PER MATCH, MEN'S WORLD CUP

Record: 5.4 goals
Record holder: Hungary
Year record was set: 1954
Former record holder: Poland
How long previous record stood:
16 years

HIGH-SCORING WORLD CUP

Hungary's Sándor Kocsis scored 11 goals at the 1954 tournament. This set the record for most goals scored by a player at one World Cup at the time.

RECORD-BREAKING MATCHES

One World Cup match can turn any team into a soccer legend. The tournament's fast-paced action makes each face-off between teams a must-watch event.

Switzerland and Austria played an action-packed match at the 1954 Men's Cup. After starting the match 0–3, Austria recovered the lead. The team went on to defeat Switzerland 7–5. Austria's epic **comeback** became the highest-scoring World Cup match ever!

HIGHEST-SCORING CUP

The 1954 Men's Cup was the highest-scoring Cup ever. An average of 5.4 goals were made per match!

MOST COMBINED GOALS SCORED IN A GAME, MEN'S WORLD CUP

Record: 12 goals

Record holders:
Austria and Switzerland

Year record was set: 1954

Former record holders:
Brazil and Poland (1938) and
Hungary and Germany (1954)

How long previous record stood:
16 years

MOST CARDS IN ONE GAME, MEN'S WORLD CUP

Record: 20 cards
Record holders:
Portugal and Netherlands
Year record was set: 2006
Former record holders:
Cameroon and Germany
How long previous record stood:
4 years

Portugal and the Netherlands were on their worst behavior at the 2006 Men's Cup. Rough tackles and dirty kicks caused the referee to give out a record 20 cards during the match. Sixteen **yellow cards** and four **red cards** were flashed by the end!

Germany achieved the biggest **blowout** at the 2007 Women's Cup. Superstars Birgit Prinz and Sandra Smisek scored **hat tricks** to help the team crush Argentina 11–0. No team has ever scored as many points in a World Cup match before!

BIGGEST BLOWOUT, WOMEN'S WORLD CUP

Record: 11-0
Record holder: Germany
Year record was set: 2007
Previous record holders:
Sweden (1991) and Norway (1995)
How long previous record stood: 16 years

U.S. men's goalie Tim Howard had an unforgettable match at the 2014 Men's Cup. Pelted by shot after shot from Belgium, Howard recorded 16 **saves** during the faceoff. The U.S. lost 1–2, but Howard walked away with the all-time saves record!

MOST SAVES IN A GAME, MEN'S WORLD CUP

Record: 16 saves
Record holder: Tim Howard
Year record was set: 2014
Former record holder:
Ramón Quiroga
How long previous record stood:
36 years

Carli Lloyd

The U.S. women's team won the 2015 Cup with ease. They stunned Japan with five goals, the most ever during a women's final. Four of these goals alone came during the first 16 minutes of the match!

MOST GOALS SCORED IN A FINAL, WOMEN'S WORLD CUP

Record: 5 goals

Record holder: United States

Year record was set: 2015

Former record holders: multiple teams tied

How long previous record stood: 24 years

RECORD-BREAKING PLAYS

Players can enter the record books in the blink of an eye at the World Cup. Fans love to go wild at every great goal or save. Each play is remembered as an incredible feat.

It took Turkey's Hakan Sükür 10.8 seconds to score against South Korea at the 2002 Men's Cup. Sükür's teammate stole the ball right after **kickoff**. Sükür then launched it into the net, scoring the fastest goal from kickoff in Men's Cup history!

FASTEST GOAL FROM KICKOFF, MEN'S WORLD CUP

Record: 10.8 seconds
Record holder: Hakan Sükür
Year record was set: 2002
Former record holder: Václav Mašek
How long previous record stood:
40 years

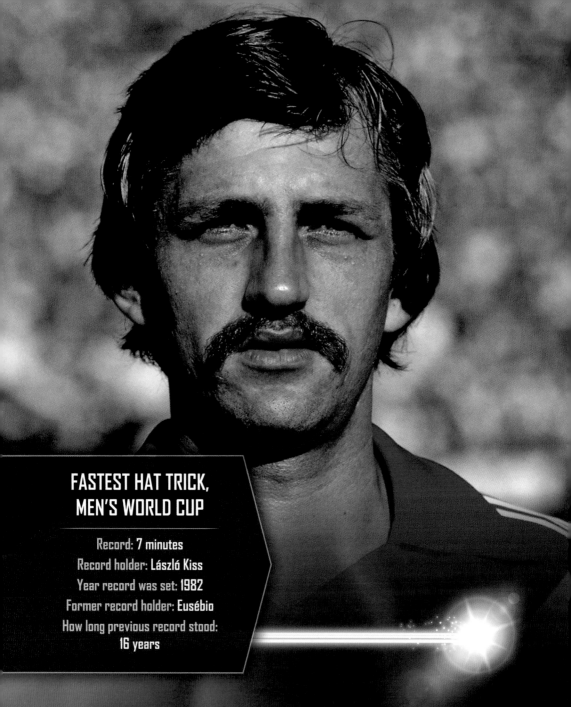

FASTEST HAT TRICK, MEN'S WORLD CUP

Record: 7 minutes
Record holder: László Kiss
Year record was set: 1982
Former record holder: Eusébio
How long previous record stood:
16 years

Hungary's László Kiss entered the game as a **substitute** against El Salvador at the 1982 Men's Cup. He quickly surprised everyone! Kiss scored three goals in seven minutes, the fastest hat trick ever at the Cup.

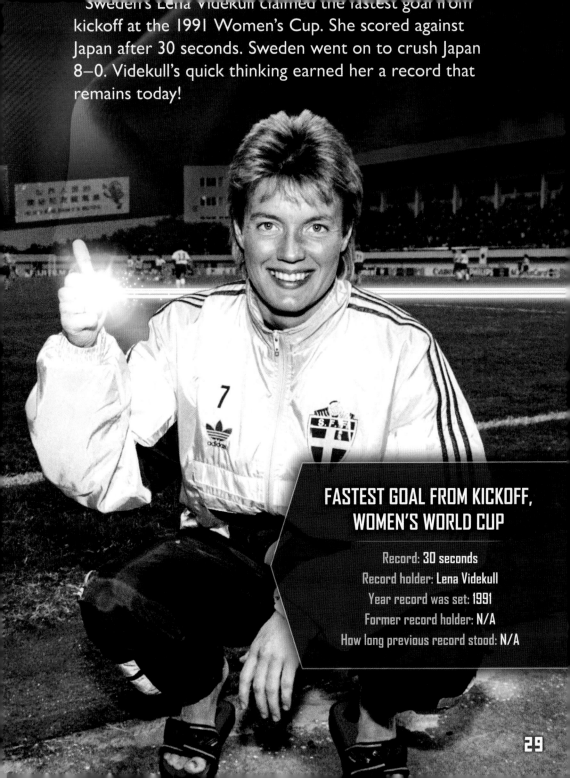

Sweden's Lena Videkull claimed the fastest goal from kickoff at the 1991 Women's Cup. She scored against Japan after 30 seconds. Sweden went on to crush Japan 8–0. Videkull's quick thinking earned her a record that remains today!

FASTEST GOAL FROM KICKOFF, WOMEN'S WORLD CUP

Record: **30 seconds**
Record holder: Lena Videkull
Year record was set: 1991
Former record holder: N/A
How long previous record stood: N/A

GLOSSARY

blowout—a match in which one team wins by scoring many more points than the other team

comeback—when a team overcomes a losing score to win a match

consecutive—one right after the other

goalkeepers—players in soccer who protect their team's goal and keep the ball from entering it

goals—scores in soccer; a player scores a goal by sending the ball into the other team's net.

hat tricks—plays in which one player scores three goals

header—a pass or shot of the ball using the player's head

kickoff—the kick of the ball that starts a soccer match

penalty kick—after certain fouls, a clear shot at the goal with no defenders in the way other than the goalie

red cards—second penalties on a player; players who get red cards must leave the match.

saves—times a goalkeeper stops the ball from going into the net for a goal

shutouts—games in which the losing team does not score

streaks—series of events that happen one right after the other

substitute—a player who takes the place of another player in a game

tournament—a contest between competitors where each is trying to be the winner

yellow cards—warnings given to a player for a penalty

TO LEARN MORE

AT THE LIBRARY

Crisfield, Deborah W. *The Everything Kids' Soccer Book: Rules, Techniques, and More About Your Favorite Sport!* Avon, Mass.: Adams Media, 2015.

Hurley, Michael. *World Cup Nations.* Chicago, Ill.: Capstone Raintree, 2014.

Peterson, Megan Cooley. *Soccer's Biggest Moments.* Mankato, Minn.: Black Rabbit Books, 2018.

ON THE WEB

Learning more about soccer records is as easy as 1, 2, 3.

1. Go to www.factsurfer.com.

2. Enter "soccer records" into the search box.

3. Click the "Surf" button and you will see a list of related web sites.

With factsurfer.com, finding more information is just a click away.

INDEX

The images in this book are reproduced through the courtesy of: Jamie Sabau/ Getty Images, front cover; Doug Pensinger/ Getty Images, p. 4; Gilbert lundt/ Getty Images, p. 5; Clive Rose/ Getty Images, p. 6 (inset); Robert Cianflone/ Getty Images, pp. 6-7; DB/ picture-alliance/ dpa/ AP Images, p. 8; Andre Pichette/ Rex Features, p. 9; Art Rickerby/ Getty Images, p. 10; Kevin C. Cox/ Getty Images, p. 11; INTERFOTO/ Alamy, p. 12; Christof Koepsel/ Getty Images, p. 13; Matthew Ashton - EMPICS/ Getty Images, p. 14 (inset); CARLO FUMAGALLI/ AP Images, pp. 14-15; Lars Baron - FIFA/ Getty Images, p. 16; Matthias Hangst/ Getty Images, p. 17; Jon Buckle - EMPICS/ Getty Images, pp. 18-19; Baumann/ ZUMA Press, p. 19 (inset); AP Images, pp. 20-21; IVAN SEKRETAREV/ AP Images, p. 22; Ronald Martinez/ Getty Images, p. 23; FRANCISCO LEONG/ Getty Images, p. 24; Christopher Morris - Corbis/ Getty Images, p. 25; PA Images/ Alamy, pp. 26-27, 28; Bildbyr•N/ ZUMA Press, p. 29.